The
Mad Dogologist's
Illustrated
Dictionary

Book One

The Mad Dogologist

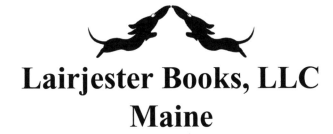

Lairjester Books, LLC
Maine

A portion of the proceeds from the sale of this book
will be donated to animal rescue organizations and shelters,
including Harvest Hills Animal Shelter
and Dachshund Rescue of North America.

In memory *of all the dog spirits, subtle heart thieves and clever sorcerers alike,*
who have magically touched my heart, rendering it fertile ground. Indeed,
this work was created with the help of my canine muses and my human mother from the Other Side!

*This book is **dedicated** to all dogs, especially the following:*
Hattie-Jean the Dachshund Queen of the Subterranean World, Lucy May,
Suzy Cue, The Budster, Kaiser (a.k.a "Special K" and "Baby Jo! Baby Jo!"),
Rudger, Clyde, *and **Tilly.***
*It is also dedicated to **Gerald E. Giroux,** whose admiration of my*
"quirkoplenus" qualities is quite perplexing.

In honor *of **Danielle Eifler,** DVM, Diplomate ACVIM (Neurology), one of the finest practitioners*
with not just a heart of gold, but the heart of a canine--Hattie-Jean will vouch for that!--and
a critical eye that rarely misses a presenting symptom. Truly a soul "paw picked" by Dog Spirit
to serve in the BEST interest of all animals on Planet Earth.

*This work is a **celebration** of my friendship with*
Susie Yates, North Carolina Representative of Dachshund Rescue of North America, *and **Dean Clark,***
both with whom I credit the inspiration to adopt physically challenged and geriatric canines.

*I **thank** the members of my Writers and Artists Group.*
*In addition, I thank my loyal friend and former colleague **Marilee Osier,** whose*
knowledge of Latin and etymology proved helpful with the development of several entries.

*Further, I must **acknowledge** all who have influenced and developed my*
bark, howl, and whine, not to mention my gait, prance, and frolic.

Appenormous

\ˈa-pə̇-ˈnȯr-məs\ *adj* [disputed origins, perh. fr. L *appetitus*, L *enormis* (fr. *e* out of, out + *norma* rule]

1 : exceeding the usual rule, norm, or measure of appetite <The *appenormous* canine was gifted in the paranormal act of making human fodder vanish from countertops without so much as a leap or bound.> **2 :** maximizing the benefits resultant from the absence of an appetitive shutoff valve
3 : displaying an insatiable desire for "sweet taters and badger meat"
4 : defying a rational explanation of temptation while in the magical presence of succulent edibles <Using psychic phenomenon, unexplainable to humankind, the *appenormous* hound employed powerful energy techniques to control human hand/eye/mouth coordination, altering--in mid-transit--the ingestive destination of coveted delights.>

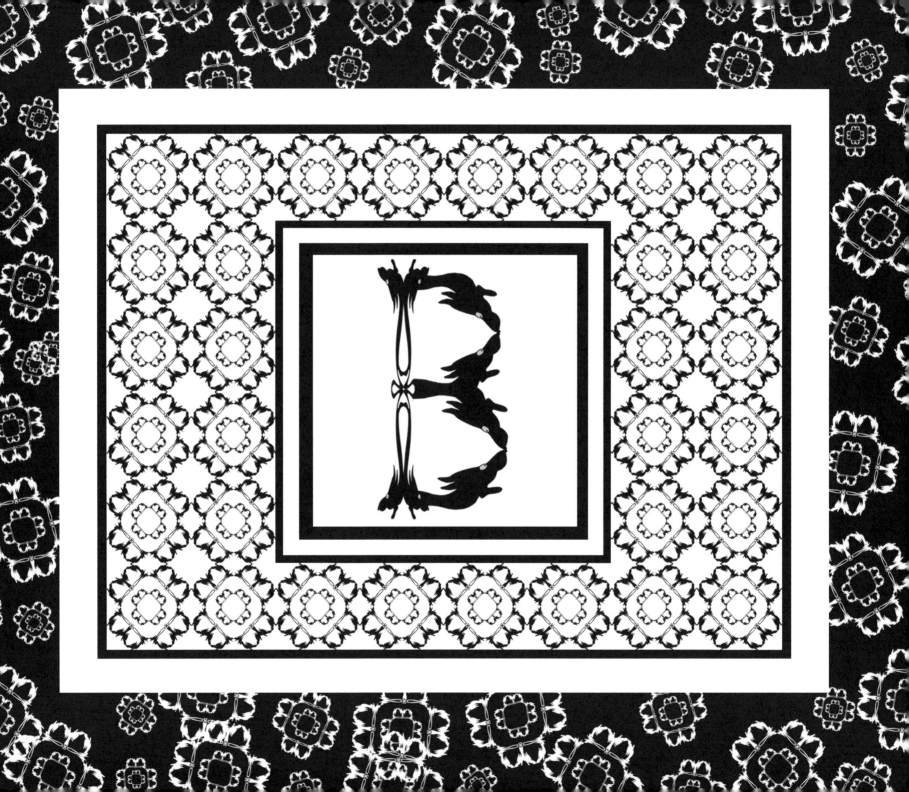

Badgerosis

\ˈba-jər-ō-səs\ *n* [disputed origins, prob. fr. *badge* + *-er*; fr. the white mark on its forehead, Gk *-ōsis* during the Badgerlicious Period] **1 :** a canine preoccupation with certain strong sturdily built burrowing mammals constituting two genera of the family Mustelidae <The hound afflicted with *badgerosis* bayed with uncontrollable excitation upon detecting the odoriferous scent of the formidable badger.> **2 :** a severe obsessive disorder with a poor prognosis for the vast majority of canines and a hopeless prognosis for the dachshund <"Hattie-Jean the Dachshund Queen of the Subterranean World" flat-out refused enrollment in an experimental research program where geneticists sought to isolate the gene responsible for *badgerosis* and to, once and for all, eliminate the disorder.>

Canineoid

\ˈkā-ˌnīn-ˌȯid\ *n* -s [L *caninus*, L *-oïdes*, fr. Gk *-oeidēs*] **1** : a rare, playful humanlike creature with a tail and a personality resembling that of the canine <Anthropologists strongly dispute that a *canineoid* was the product of an interspecies entanglement initiated by an indiscriminating canine during the Canidaeous Period.> **2** : a human (of questionable origins) born with a vertebral deformation and a personality disorder <Although the vast majority of behavioral scientists argue that the *canineoid* is definitively rooted in mythological origins, a group of Freudian adherents espouse that such a human does, indeed, exist and that the personality disorder remains (and must be treated aggressively) even after amputation of the tail.>

Dogologist

\ˈdȯg-ˈä-lə-jəst\ *n* -s [prob. fr. ME *dog*, *dogge*, fr. OE *docga* + *-ologist*] **1** : one possessed by the spirited charm and feisty finesse of the dog <The Mad *Dogologist* continuously sketched repetitive geometric dogsigns, all the while fancying herself the M.C. Escher of the canine art world.> **2** : one whose stream of consciousness is ever invaded by images of the magical Canis Familiaris beast **3** : one who is prone to auditory hallucinosis, hearing barks <Roused from the depths of sleep, The Mad *Dogologist* (convinced that Dog Spirit had summoned) leapt from her lair to follow the incessant baying, which evaded direction, leaving her spinning in circles.>

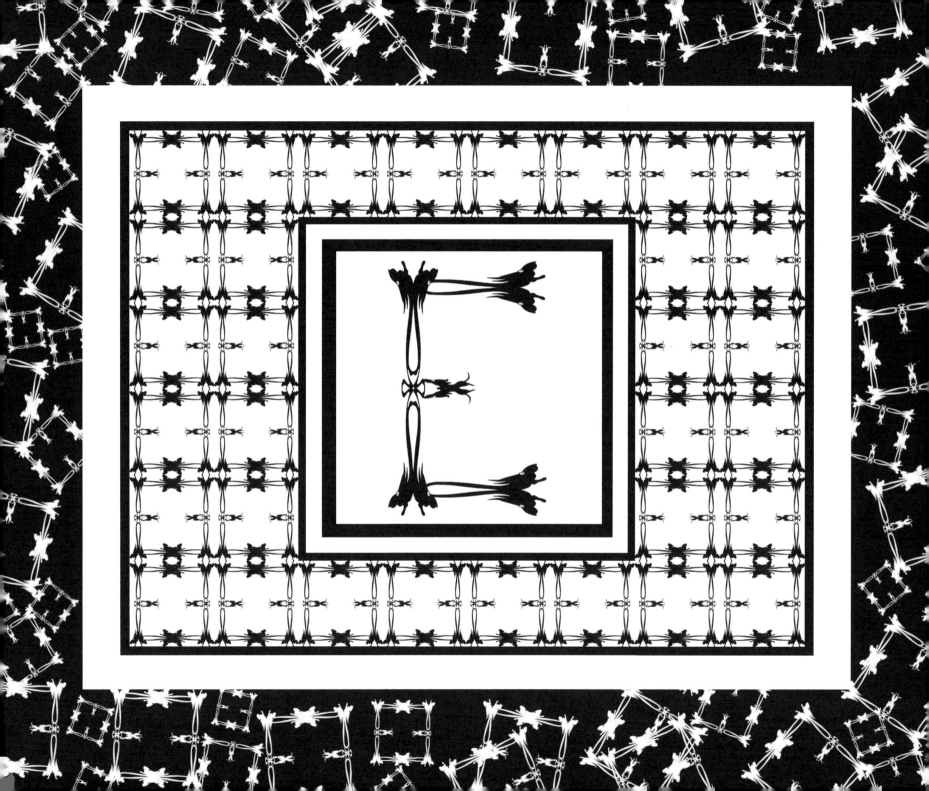

Exuberitionist

\ig-ˈzü-bər-i-shə-nist\ *n* -s [disputed origins, perh. fr. F *exubérance*, ISV *exhibition* + *-ist*] : a joyfully unrestrained and enthusiastic canine : one that is extremely or excessively high-spirited and uninhibited <Sparky, the *exuberitionist*, mischievously sat beside his human on a park bench, where he exposed his full exuberancy to every passerby whose head turned his way.> <At the "Thirteenth Annual Animal Behavior Conference" in Berserkley, California, attendees flocked to the daylong workshop titled "Innocent Canine *Exuberitionist* or Menacing Pest: How *You* Can Tell the Difference.">

Feistorama

\ˈfīs(t)-ə-ra-mə \ *n* -s [prob. fr. *feisty*, Gk *horama* sight]
: a lively festival where rambunctious canines act out their untamed friskiness and exuberancy through vocal and acrobatic performances <At the "Hounds Rule *Feistorama*" the lead howler of the Worst Wiener Blues Band bayed--with frantic zest--the demanding passage: "Ain't no badger, leave it DOWN in the hole!" from the song "Better Get Your Meat Right, Honey!"> <With the ease of an experienced subterranean invader, the canine contortionist performed the act: "Dive Way Down, Don't Come Up Empty-Mouthed" at the annual *feistorama*.>

Genusfrolickus

\ˈjē-nəs-ˈfrä-li-kəs\ *n, pl* **genusfrolicki** [prob. fr.
L *genus* class, kind, MD *vrolijc*, fr. *vro* happy, joyful] **:** a group
marked by the common characteristic of ecstatic frolic **:** a group
capable of including subgroups <The family Canidae is well-
established as a subgroup of the classification *genusfrolickus*,
characterized as being full of fun or mirth.> <Possessed by the
Great Spirit of Play, the canines (epitomes of *genusfrolickus*) joyfully
frisked about the open fields of the sunny uplands, where they jumped
through tall blades of grass and caught enticing smells on the steady,
gentle breeze, all the while waiting for the scent of the rare
Golden Woodchuck.>

Heartthievery

\\ˈhärt-ˈthē-və-rē\\ *n* [disputed origins, prob. fr. ME *hert*, fr. OE *heorte*; akin to OHG *herza* heart, ME *theef*] **:** the art of stealing one's heart (love and affections), especially secretly and as if by magic or spiritual intervention <Kaiser (a.k.a. "Special K") committed *heartthievery* instantaneously upon looking into the brown eyes of The Mad Dogologist, who immediately became charmed by his humble demeanor and endearing ways, his unusually long nose and bowed legs, and his honesty and forthrightness--a true beauty beyond measure, a qualifyingly rare angel.>

Irresistocrat

\ˌir-i-ˈzis-tō-ˌkrat\ *n* -s [disputed origins, prob. fr. ME *ir-*, ME *resisten*, fr. L *resistere*, F *-crate* power] **1** : a canine that is impossible to resist successfully : one that is superior to opposition <The savvy *irresistocrat* waltzed into the courtroom, subpoena in paw, to give overwhelmingly persuasive testimony regarding a high-speed chase involving two hounds and a menacing jack rabbit.> **2** : a pact appointee with the authoritative specialization to render humans incapable of resisting canine charm <The *irresistocrat* visited the Dog House in Wienington to persuade President F. D. Woofer (a staunch supporter) that vital legislation in the interest of all animals must be passed to protect basic rights, especially of dogs.>

Jinkdographer

\jiŋk-'dȯ-grə-fə(r)\ *n* -s [disputed origins, unknown *jink,* ME *dog,* F *grapher*] : a canine engaging in the composition and often the instruction of jinkdography (the art of representing quick moves and sudden turns using signs) <Lucille, a downright vicious *jinkdographer*, scratched into the dirt the signs for a brutally complex series of jink maneuvers to accompany the first movement *Allegro Pazzia* of Dogzart's Symphony No. 113 in C Major ("Chasing Scents on Hurricane Winds").>

Kleptogrubniac

\ˌklep-tə-ˈgrəb-nē-ˌak\ *n* -s [NL, fr. *klept-* + LL *grubniac*]

1 : a canine afflicted with the persistent neurotic impulse to steal raw meaty bones, chipmunk carcasses, and other remains usually believed to have symbolic meaning associated with elevated status <Hunger was not the motive behind the *kleptogrubniac's* gristly raid of her very own pack's stash; still, beta culprit Suzy Cue ceremoniously consumed the entrails of one chipmunk to mark her stand among the mighty alpha hunters.> **2 :** a canine with an obsession to artfully display exhibits of the criminal act--impulsive theft <The smooth-operating double dappled *kleptogrubniac* fancied herself a museum curator, arranging lifeless prey into thought-provoking exhibits.>

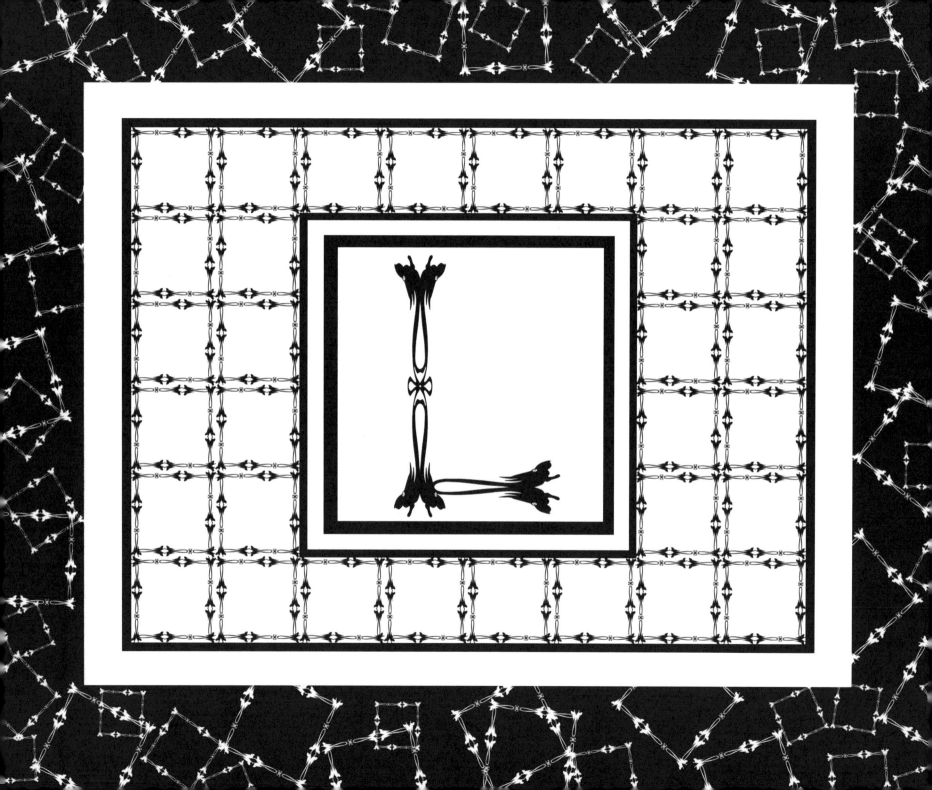

Lairjester

\\'ler-'jes-tər\\ *n* -s [ME *lair, leir,* fr. OE *leger*; akin to OHG *legar* bed, alter. of ME *gestour,* fr. *gesten* to tell a tale + *-our* -or] : a canine entertainer given to howling out jests and performing acts (about the frailties of humans) intended to provoke laughter from the pack, bunking down wildly in the lair <Before a lively pack of canines (bellies up, legs kicking), the *lairjester* sparked her audience when she howled out, "Talk about being olfactorily challenged: our deficient humans can't even smell (or positively identify) our fragrant excrement--right on the bottoms of their shoes!-- until they've done a visual inspection and taken a close-up whiff or two of "Specimen A" (by then tracked *all* over the crime scene).>

Maestrobeggar

\ˈmī-strō-ˈbe-gər\ *n* -s [It, lit., master, fr. L *magister* teacher, ME *beggare*, *beggere*, fr. *beggen* to beg + *-are*] : a canine that teaches the fine art of begging; *esp* **:** a master that holds vast knowledge about begging styles (e.g., humble, passive aggressive, interactive) <The old *maestrobeggar* inspired his followers with words of great wisdom: "Never look *at* your human, look right through 'em, and not only with your eyes, but with all your heart and soul!"> <In her self-help guide, <u>Meditative Exercises for Ineffectual Beggars</u>, *maestrobeggar* Hatsfield MacGregor advised her audience to envision humans making peace offerings to canines by surrendering their T-bone steaks.>

Napmeister

\\ˈnap-ˈmī-stə(r)\\ *n* -s [ME *nap, nappe,* fr. *nappen,* G *meister* master] **1 :** a hound that has mastered the art form of napping <The *napmeister* tootled over to her feather bed; sniffed the retro kitty fabric; climbed into the center, vigorously scratching the genuine fleece lining; and twirled three times to the left, four times to the right, and two times back to the left before seizing her squeaky blue bone, rolling over onto her back, and closing her eyes.> **2 :** a pack alpha that serves as master of nap ceremonies <The *napmeister* awarded each graduate with a diploma, identifying the level of distinction: summa nap laude, stage IV; magna nap laude, stage III; nap laude, stages II and I; and nap wachtmeister, stage D (deficient).>

Omniwurst

\äm-'ni-'würst\ *n* -s [ME *omni-* all, G *-wurst* sausage] **1** : a sausage dog (dachshund) whose shapeliness is undisputably recognized as the all-American ball park symbol of wurst excellence <No ball park is alive without the savor of a succulent *omniwurst* stimulating the stands with aromatic irresistibility.> **2** : the dachshund breed, universally accepted as having the most flavorfully spiced temperament of the "wurst" family <Bratwurst, brockwurst, weisswurst, only the *omniwurst* takes the coveted "Golden Mustard Award" and holds its own among the top scoring players at the Wurst Hall Of Fame.>

Pawsytraction

\ˈpȯ-zē-ˈtrak-shən\ *n* [ME, fr. MF *poue*, ML *traction*]
: the act of drawing or pulling a body by a quadruped (with claws) using cardio-muscular motive power <The calculating canine with *pawsytraction* took the curves at Bad Badger Burrow as though an Austin Mini Twinny Cooper roaring around White House Corner at LeMans or cornering the hairpin curves of Nürbergring.> <When creating the canine with *pawsytraction*, The Great Designer had to pay special attention to gear ratios, braking abilities, engine displacement, independent suspension, and--above and beyond all--weight distribution.>

Quirkoplenus

\ˈkwərk-ō-ˈple-nəs\ *adj* [disputed origins, unknown *quirk*, perh. fr. the Wackocaninus Period, L *plenus* full of] : having an abundance of peculiarity related to action, behavior, or bearing <The *quirkoplenus* pup was notorious about the neighborhood for her fastidious chipmunk designs, which decorated many a granite back step, her preferred canvas.> <An "old dog" at coaching, *quirkoplenus* Casey gestured a series of signals (nose twitch to the left, followed by a right rear leg kick, followed by a full tilt tail twirl) to communicate to her human players the message: "Better serve Happiness brand (canned) Sweet Taters and Badger Meat variety--if you want to score big-time and know what's good for you!">

Rascalization

\ˈras-kə-lə-ˈzā-shən\ *n* -s [Me *rascal* + *-ization*]

1 : the metamorphotic process of changing into an unpredictably mischievous canine <As Manuel's beaming humans vaingloriously watched him receive "Best of Show" at the Wienminster Dog Show, the high-spirited dachshund picked up the scent of wienerwurst on one of the judge's meaty digits, causing immediate *rascalization*, resulting in a multi-digital disaster of unparalleled proportions.> **2 :** a process which results in an inexplicable metamorphosis of character <To experience the thrill of entering Rascaldom, obedience champion Mathila understood that she must complete full *rascalization*; still, she lamented over the wisdom of gently removing her human's savored T-bone steak from the hibachi, where it slowly barbecued over hickory wood.>

Shrillprano

\\ˈshril-ˈpra-nō \ *n* -s [disputed origins, prob. fr. ME *shrille*, It *sopra* above + *-ano* -an] **1 :** the highest, most penetrating canine voice part (hound classification) in 7-part mixed harmony (or disharmony), typically belonging to the smaller breeds <Roberta was a well-known *shrillprano* capable of eardrum-pulsing performances, where--as though a seasoned gymnast on an agility course--she easily achieved notes above fourth C.>
2 : a canine singer having gained notoriety through a sharp insistence on being heard <The vindictive *shrillprano* used her vocal prowess to a punitive end, disciplining human delinquents for deficiencies in the areas of food service and affection.>

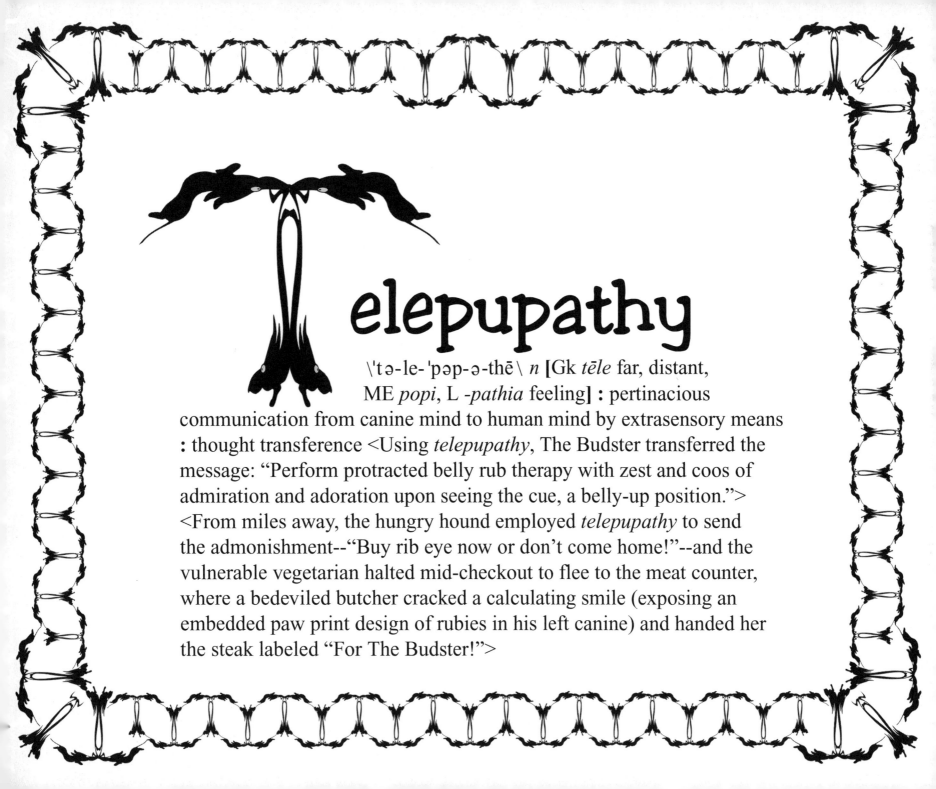

Telepupathy

\ˈtə-le-ˈpəp-ə-thē\ *n* [Gk *tēle* far, distant, ME *popi*, L *-pathia* feeling] **:** pertinacious communication from canine mind to human mind by extrasensory means **:** thought transference <Using *telepupathy*, The Budster transferred the message: "Perform protracted belly rub therapy with zest and coos of admiration and adoration upon seeing the cue, a belly-up position."> <From miles away, the hungry hound employed *telepupathy* to send the admonishment--"Buy rib eye now or don't come home!"--and the vulnerable vegetarian halted mid-checkout to flee to the meat counter, where a bedeviled butcher cracked a calculating smile (exposing an embedded paw print design of rubies in his left canine) and handed her the steak labeled "For The Budster!">

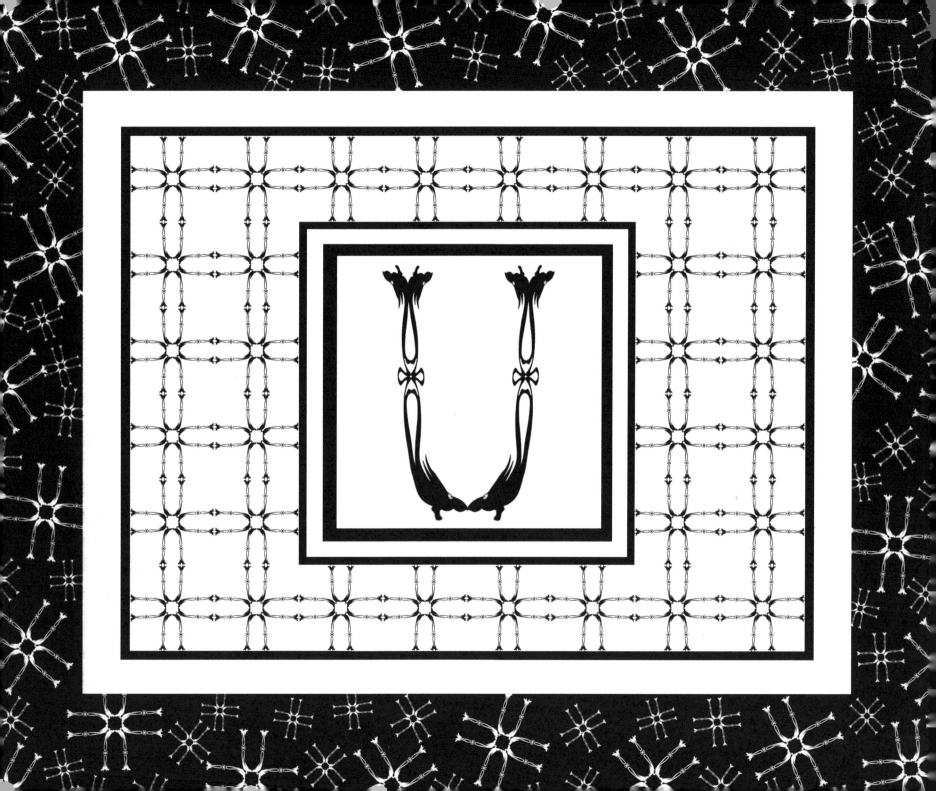

Ultraproboscis

\ˈəl-trə-prō-ˈbä-sə̇s\ *n* -es [L, fr. *ultra* beyond, L, fr. Gk *proboskis*, fr. *pro-* + *boskein* to feed] : an unusually long canine muzzle with an exceptionally prominent proboscis at the end <Senior dog "Baby Jo! Baby Jo!" was comically admired for his *ultraproboscis*, which he used to track all activity of his humans and his felicitous friends, both feline and canine.> <Using the divine powers endowed upon his *ultraproboscis*, "Special K" tracked his way to his Maker's side, where his soul rests in eternal peace and where he never loses "track" of those who loved him dearly, especially The Mad Dogologist.>

Vociferoso

\vō-ˌsif-ər-ˈwō-sō\ *n* -s [disputed origins, prob. fr. LL *vocifer* cry aloud + (fr. It *oso*), It *virtuoso*] : a talented pooch that excels in the artistic form of political oratory <The charged *vociferosos* protested with such vehemence about the quality of commercial kibble that human spectators fled toward emergency exits only to find that packs of insistent canine activists had blocked them off with sacks of cornmeal based *human* kibble, specifically the *specially* formulated brand "Then You Eat It!" (labeled **Not Fit for Canine Consumption**) imported from Shangri-La.>

Wientripetal

\ˈwēn-ˈtri-pə-tᵊl\ *adj* [disputed origins, perh. fr. G *wiener*, L *petere* to go toward, seek] : moving, proceeding, or acting in a direction toward a wienerdog <The calculating wienerdog employed intense *wientripetal* energy to constrain the movement of his humans and to keep them centered around him at all times of night and day.> <The Mad Dogologist was keenly aware of the dangers imminent in entering the energy field of a self-centered dachshund suffering from a severe case of separation anxiety, especially during the spring and fall equinoxes when the mysterious powers of nature exponentially increased the strength of the *wientripetal* force.>

Xenodogphile

\\ˈzenə-ˈdȯg-ˌfīl\\ *n* -s [LL, fr. Gk, fr. *xenos* stranger, ME *dog, dogge,* fr. OE *docga,* F -*phile,* fr. Gk *philos* beloved] : a human preferring the friendship and companionship of dogs <Without reservation, the caritative canines welcomed the *xenodogphile* into their pack in spite of her general disregard for species practices, such as the proper way to greet newcomers and the art of fine grooming.> <Leaving her all-American, middle-class family had never been a decision involving lamentation, for the *xenodogphile* had heard the call of the "Mighty Pack" since birth.>

Youthfulizer

\ˈyüth-fə-ˌlī-zər\ *n* -s [prob. fr. ME *youthe*, fr. OE *geoguth*; akin to MD *joget* youth + *-ful* + *-izer*]

1 : a canine with divine abilities used to heal the ailing spirit and to restore a sense of emotional well-being <The alternative medicine practitioner ordered her patient to spend one to two hours each day in the presence of at least one *youthfulizer*.> **2** : a wienerdog (with an "all natural" casing) prescription concocted to lighten the heart and to generate ecstatic happiness <Two... three... four... it's impossible to overdose on the number of *youthfulizers*, and there are no adverse side effects whatsoever!>

Zeroplate

\\'zē-rō-'plāt\ *n* -s [F *zéro*, fr. ML *zephirum*, fr. Ar *sifr* empty, OF *plate*]: a plate (literary or culinary) that is absent of food (for mind or for body) <Although arriving at *zeroplate* with gauges registering full, appenormous human connoisseurs of the canine world and of linguistic play found themselves debating the definition and etymology of the word *satiation*.> <After thoroughly ingesting the contents of <u>The Mad Dogologist's Illustrated Dictionary, Book One</u> and coming to a screeching halt at *zeroplate*, the voluminous appetite of canine enthusiasts for literary fodder left them hungering for more: <u>The Mad Dogologist's Illustrated Dictionary, Book Two</u>, coming soon.>

It is with immense **gratitude** *that I recognize the following dedicated individuals
in the field of veterinary medicine at the Sacopee Veterinary Clinic,
Maine Veterinary Referral Center, and Portland Veterinary Specialists:*
Mark Beever, *DVM, whose dedication to Rudger will never be forgotten;*
Laurie Cook, *DVM, Diplomate ACVIM (Neurology), whose diagnostic abilities, surgical skills,
and home care support recommendations are responsible for Lucy May walking today;*
Alan Potthoff, *DVM, Diplomate ACVIM (Neurology), a visionary for advanced veterinary medicine, whose
foresight has brought essential services to the State of Maine, and a patient educator who taught me to
express the urinary bladders of neurologically impaired animals (my greatest accomplishment to date);*
Katie Marles, *Veterinary Technician, whose knowledge of her patients and
unwavering dedication to each of them rank her among the best;*
Nancy Wade, *Veterinary Technician, whose expertise and kind words instill confidence and a sense of security;*
Andrea Scasserra, *DVM, whose love for The Budster keeps him rolling;*
Gail D. Mason, *DVM, MA, DACVIM, whose love surrounded "Special K" when he crossed the bridge to
the Other Side and whose nurturing nature comforted me when I arrived ten minutes
after my dear boy had boarded a heaven-bound 747 (on a full tummy at that!);*
Betty Jo Harmon, *Client Specialist, whose sensitivity to clients is admirable
and whose listening skills are remarkable;*
Heidi Ludewig, *Veterinary Technician, whose dedication is off the scale;*
Debbie Dearth (DD), *Veterinary Technician, whose sense of humor lurks by the abyss;*
Crystal Waite, *Veterinary Technician, whose sense of humor rivals that of* **DD**;
Mary Ann Bradeen, *Receptionist, whose ability to find a slot in the busiest of schedules is uncanny;*
Blanche Collomy,*Veterinary Technician, whose sincerity is the ultimate;*
Kelly Hand, *Veterinary Technician, whose pack amazingly exceeds mine in size;*
Ellen Paine-Dimond, *Receptionist, whose words of encouragement are reinforcing;*
and **ALL THE OTHER FINE SOULS** *who have enriched my life by providing
excellent care for my loved ones (my apologies for not mentioning each of you by name).*

.